THE SALES INTERVIEW

by

SCOTT ANTHONY RHEAULT

Table of Contents

Introduction iii

What Are We Looking For? 1

Building a Résumé with Impact. 13

Preparation: The Key to Interview Success 27

Secrets to a Successful Phone Screen. 43

Face-to-Face Interviews 47

Behavioral Interviews 61
Targeted Selection®
Sample Behavioral Questions. 66

Sample Questions 71

A Day in the Field 77

Always & Never: The Do's and Don'ts
of Interviewing. 81

Resources: Where to Find What You Need 87

"Success doesn't come to you, you go to it."
—*Marva Collins*

FORWARD

By Karen Halkovic
President, Biotech Pharma Recruiters, Inc.

Do you ever ask yourself why some interviews go so well and others fall flat? Was it the way the interviewer asked the questions, or was it the way I answered them? Did I have enough experience? Was I truly prepared? Did I focus on results?

The ultimate goal of any interview is to land the position. You only have one chance to make a positive impression. Today, there are a plethora of outstanding candidates. The pharmaceutical, medical, and biotech market is highly competitive. Organizations and hiring managers have become diligent in their interviewing and hiring practices. Research shows for each open sales position one hundred to one hundred fifty resumes are submitted to human resources departments. Needless to say, the marketplace is very competitive.

While I do not consider myself an expert, I have spent the past thirty years in the pharmaceutical industry, fifteen of which have been in recruiting. So many outstanding candidates have failed the interview process, not because they are unqualified, but because they do not know how to interview correctly. They are unprepared and have never been given the secrets to the interview process. Benjamin Franklin said it best; By failing to prepare, you are preparing to fail.

After spending hours coaching candidates, I am thrilled to have a "how-to" guide to refer to my candidates. *The Sales Interview* was written by a twenty-eight-year industry veteran, industry insider and hiring manager. Never again will any candidate have to ask, the questions, "I wonder what they are looking for, how should I prepare, and what should I expect?"

In *The Sales Interview*, Scott has written a comprehensive, step-by-step resource for a successful interview. He gives you the tools in a well-defined, easy-to-execute format. You will come out of each and every interview saying to yourself, "I hit a home run."

I know you will find this guide an essential part of your job search. Good luck!

"The greatest potential for control tends to exist at the point where action takes place."

—*Louis Allen*

INTRODUCTION

I wrote *The Sales Interview* because there are never two candidates with equal qualifications, *never*. There is always a candidate who is better prepared, more confident, and better able to present his or her skills and abilities. There is always a candidate who can best demonstrate how his or her behavior will transfer to future performance. Pharmaceutical, medical, surgical, and biotech sales positions are among the most competitive of any industry. Regardless of the economy, sales positions in the medical field remain lucrative and stable. Think about the customer: doctors, nurses, pharmacists, surgeons, technicians. They are highly educated. They demand and expect the best from sales professionals. The pharmaceutical and health care industry has been and will continue to redefine itself, however opportunities remain strong for the right individual. It is estimated the top growth industries over the next fifteen to twenty years will be health care-related. With demand comes opportunity; with opportunity comes responsibility.

I wrote this guide because I have been disappointed and frustrated too many times by qualified people who are simply unprepared for the interview process. I have worked for small organizations as well as Fortune 500 companies. While there were countless résumé-writing and interviewing resources, I realized there wasn't a comprehensive resource specific to the pharmaceutical, medical device, surgical or biotech industry. By and large, our industry uses the same methods to screen and hire. The techniques are tried, true, deliberate and time tested. I wrote this guide as an "industry insider." I know the process, methods and techniques because I am part of the industry, and I use them each time I interview and make a hiring decision.

The Sales Interview was written for *all* candidates regardless of experience. The principles are universal and easily applied to sales and non-sales positions. Interviewing is not easy. Every candidate needs a competitive edge. Take the time and follow the principles outlined in this guide. They are proven to work, and while there is never a guarantee, the landscape is too competitive to leave to chance. You must take advantage of every resource available. My hope is that *The Sales Interview* will yield the best return on your time and your investment. The investment is your career.

The following best practices, tips, and recommendations are a culmination of real-life experiences taken from hundreds of people I have interviewed over the course of my twenty- eight year career. I purposely did not write a narrative guide. Sales people respond to and execute bullet-point direction. This guide is just that. The suggestions and guidelines are real, universal, and based on practical industry experience. The principles outlined in this workbook are easily applied to pharmaceutical, medical device, surgical and biotech sales positions. In fact, the majority of the material in this workbook can be applied to all outside sales positions regardless of industry.

Congratulations on taking the first step by purchasing and reading this guide. But don't just read the guide. Use it as it was intended: as a workbook. Plan, prepare, and execute. Take notes and highlight critical points. Challenge yourself to be better prepared than any other time in your life. The chapters in the book reflect the order in the hiring process. Take a methodical approach and follow the steps one by one. You have been given "insider" information. There is no need to guess or take chances. Never again will you say, "I wish I knew" or "I should have done things differently."

Good luck and much success.

"What I am looking for is not out there, it is in me."

-Helen Keller

WHAT ARE WE LOOKING FOR?

Now more than ever, it's important to know from the start what it is sales managers are looking for. Despite what you may hear from friends, family or health-care professionals, there are specific skills, abilities and behaviors (competencies) that we look for. The characteristics discussed in this chapter are not exhaustive but an overview of the most desirable traits and competencies needed for pharmaceutical, medical device, surgical and biotech sales. The ideal candidate is able to communicate in a concise, professional manner and demonstrate excellent sales performance. Remember this premise: Past performance predicts future behavior. Managers are interested in what you have done, how you did it, and most importantly, can you do it again? A systematic analysis of your skills and abilities should precede any communication with employers. Résumés, job applications, and job interviews are most effective when you first complete a thorough skills analysis. Get to know yourself by taking a personal inventory. Skills gained from volunteer work, hobbies, education, and other life experiences should be examined in addition to those skills gained from paid work. Focus on the skill and behavior as opposed to job title or employer.

Interviewing is a rigorous and time-consuming process. Expect a minimum of two interviews, but anticipate three or four from beginning to end. Interviews are generally progressive. In other words, a first and second interview may be with a District Sales Manager, whereas a third and fourth may be with a Regional or National Sales Director. The questions may be different with each person, but the objective remains the same.

Sales managers ask behavioral or Targeted Selection® (Situation-Task-Action-Result) questions in order to identify the behavior that yielded the result. They are not interested in philosophy, generalizations, or how you should approach a situation, but rather how you have approached various situations and the results you delivered by doing so. Hiring managers are not looking for narrative dissertations. It is critical to provide specific, relevant examples for the questions asked. You must also be able to back up your results with documentation when asked. Similar to a sales call with a physician or customer, you must be able to provide a proof source when needed.

At the end of the day, sales managers hire people they trust can deliver results, increase market share, and provide financial value to the organization. The bottom line is just that, the bottom line. The entire process, from résumé review to spending a day in the field, is designed to identify your adaptive and transferable skills regardless of your current employer or level of experience.

Characteristics and Competencies
Someone who is and has demonstrated the ability to be:
energetic, personable, passionate, organized, committed, well spoken, results-oriented, true to their word, honest, ethical, self-aware,

*coachable, timely, creative, appropriate, empathic, prepared, fo-
cused, professional, smart, goal-oriented, accountable, consider-
ate, able to communicate, tenacious, conscientious, dependable,
self-monitoring, proactive, hardworking, decisive, accountable,
empathetic, analytical, responsible, motivated, flexible, self-reli-
ant, consistent, a strategic thinker, a closer, a team player, a good
listener and a leader; someone who has good business acumen,
selling skills, organizational effectiveness, and the ability to build
relationships and leverage them, and to learn and communicate
technical data; and someone who hates to lose but loves to win,
wants to develop and can analyze-strategize-execute.*

This is not an exhaustive list. Print the job description or posting from the company website. What are the characteristics
and competencies of their "ideal" candidate? **Now you know
exactly what they are looking for.**

o The entire interview process is designed to determine if
   you are the person who demonstrates the traits, skills, and
   characteristics of their ideal candidate.

o Write down examples of specific actions you have taken
   that demonstrate proficiency in each competency. Industry
   examples are best. This is extra work but well worth it.

EXAMPLE:
*analytical – used IMS physician TRx data to create a routing
plan, maximize reach and frequency on high volume customers and increase market share with those customers.*

_____

_____

_____

_____

_____

_____

_____

_____

_____

_____

_____

_____

_____

o Interviewers look for transferable skills and abilities. It is your responsibility during the interview to clearly communicate that you are the best-qualified person, that you are the person who generates results. Unfortunately, qualified people are not getting hired because of their inability to communicate during the process. Interviewers are "teasing out" the candidate's ability to support their qualifications. You must demonstrate qualifications through past performance and proven results. Can you verbalize what it took and what you did to produce your results? Be prepared to do so.

Three underlying questions of every interview:

1. Can the candidate transfer current skills and abilities to the position he or she is interviewing for and be successful?

2. Is the candidate the right fit?

3. How long will it take for the candidate to make an impact in the territory?

o Do you know your transferable skills? Acquire the job description or posting and print it. What are the skills and behaviors of the "ideal" candidate? List your skills that will transfer to the new position.

_____

_____

_____

_____

_____

_____

_____

_____

_____

_____

_____

_____

The following are examples of adaptive skills:
- Getting along and ability to work with fellow employees
- Professional telephone etiquette and technique
- Listening to and following directions
- Dependability
- Obeying safety regulations
- Ability to work independently

o Do you know your adaptive skills? Adaptive skills also may be referred to as school-to-work transition skills or basic skills necessary for acquiring and keeping a job. List your adaptive skills.

---

o List your jobs, hobbies, and interests. Start by listing every job you have ever held—full-time and part-time jobs as well as paid and unpaid jobs. List the skills you acquired in each job. Why? It is critical for the interviewer to know you have the skills even though you may not have the experience. This is especially useful for those breaking in to the industry.

_____

_____

_____

_____

_____

_____

_____

_____

_____

_____

_____

_____

_____

o If you are currently a pharmaceutical sales representative and are applying for medical device or surgical sales, be prepared to demonstrate your ability to set goals, meet objectives, close for business, and work in a high-pressure quota environment.

o Sales Managers like activity but only if it yields a result. Dinner programs, speaker events, and lunches are common practice in the industry. Hiring managers want to know why you did them and the result you attained. What was your return on investment? How do you know? How did you track progress and measure results? What did you do with the resources you were given (financial and personnel)?

o If working with a recruiter, take advantage of his or her expertise regarding the organization. Ask if other candidates have been placed. Have the recruiter compare your skills to theirs. If the recruiter is willing, conduct a role-play session with him or her.

o Often, recruiters know the hiring manager personally. They know his or her likes and dislikes. Take advantage of their insight for a competitive advantage.

> ## HIRING MANAGERS ARE LOOKING TO MAKE A CALCULATED AND PROFITABLE HIRING DECISION.

CONSIDER THE COST OF A "BAD HIRE."

LOST PRODUCTIVITY—*A new hire who produces in the bottom quarter of employees in any given position can produce between 25 percent and 600 percent less than top performers.*

REDUCED REVENUE—*If the new hire is in a revenue-generating or revenue-impact position, the loss of revenue could be significant.*

LOST INNOVATION—*Employees resistant to change may actually distract other employees.*

CUSTOMER IMPACT—*Customers recognize a weak employee. Hiring a subpar employee into a role that interfaces with customers can measurably reduce sales, customer satisfaction, and increase customer turnover.*

ERROR RATES—*Poor performers make many mistakes generating work that must be redone.*

SLOWER TIME TO MARKET—*Weak employees are slower in both their work and their thinking. As a result, they can slow the progress of the entire team.*

COMPETITIVE ADVANTAGE—*Hiring weak employees sends a message to competitors that you are getting weak.*

MORE MANAGEMENT TIME—*Weak hires are "high maintenance," requiring more coaching and concern. The time spent on weak employees can't be spent on the best employees, recognition or business planning.*

WEAK HIRES MUST BE REPLACED—*Even though weak candidates may appear to help in the short term, eventually (when their weak performance can no longer be tolerated), they will have to be replaced.*

PERFORMANCE MANAGEMENT AND TERMINATION COSTS—*Weak employees require frequent performance-management time, effort, and energy.*

HIRING MANAGER'S IMAGE IS NEGATIVELY IMPACTED—*It's well known that weak managers routinely hire weak employees. A hiring manager's image is at stake.*

REDUCED BONUSES—*For managers who hire and retain a significant percentage of weak performers, performance-bonus opportunities will be significantly reduced.*

IMPACTS ON PROMOTION—*Hiring weak employees, coupled with poor business results, will be noticed by superiors. This may limit chances of promotion.*

RESENTMENT BY COWORKERS—*Better-performing employees often resent being on the same team with weak performers. They may have to spend a significant portion of their time helping out or fixing the mistakes of weak employees, ultimately reducing their won productivity.*

LOST LEADERSHIP AND PROMOTIONAL OPPORTUNITIES—*Every weak hire is a missed opportunity for building leadership bench strength. Over the long term, the internal candidate pool for promotions will be dramatically reduced.*

INCREASED TURNOVER—*Hiring and keeping weak employees may send a message to high-quality employees that standards are being reduced and performance is no longer important. This may cause them to transfer or quit the organization altogether.*

OPPORTUNITY COSTS—*Every position taken up by a weak employee can't be filled with a great employee.*

NEGATIVE IMPACTS ON FUTURE HIRING—*When candidates meet and interact with weak employees, they may reconsider and pursue other opportunities.*

HIRING COSTS—*It costs no more to hire a better performer. The salary costs of weak hires are not lower than average employees.*

LOST AGILITY—*A weak hire cannot contribute to the competency of changing with a fast-paced environment and will slow down everyone else on the team.*

LONGER RAMP-UP TIME—*Weak new hires will require more time, taking longer for them to reach minimum levels of productivity if even possible.*

REDUCED LEARNING—*Other members of the team can't learn anything positive from weak employees, thus reducing overall team learning speed.*

A LOSS OF COMPETITIVE INTELLIGENCE—*New hires who come from direct competitors can provide you with little to no intelligence and best practices.*

MORE TRAINING IS REQUIRED—*Weak hires will require more access to training and retraining, which in addition to their lower levels of productivity, may result in them costing more than they produce.*

These are just a few reasons why organizations spend so much time, effort, energy, and money on recruiting and hiring. Hiring the right person is the most important job of a sales manager. The cost of a "bad hire" can be devastating.

"When we build, let us think that we build for ever."
—*John Ruskin*

BUILDING A RÉSUMÉ WITH IMPACT

I have reviewed hundreds, if not thousands, of résumés through the course of my career. There are only two reasons to write a résumé: to create interest and generate a phone call. Do not take your résumé for granted. Take the time to write a dynamic, accurate, honest, and results- focused résumé. Hiring managers and human resources departments receive hundreds of résumés for a single position. During a recent expansion, we received one hundred fifty résumés per territory opening. Imagine your résumé in a stack of one hundred fifty others. It must produce interest and attention through experience, but more importantly, by your results. I will always call the person with a performance-driven résumé. Remember, you are applying for a *sales* position. Sales managers focus on market share, market share growth, forecast attainment, and consistent delivery of sales results. They are not interested in reading a job description. We know what you do; we want to know what you have done—better yet, can you do it again? Basically, will your skills and abilities to deliver results transfer to the position for which you are applying?

The most common type of résumé is chronological, which highlights roles and responsibilities by employer and date. A one or two-page résumé is common and acceptable. The other type is functional, which highlights a person's career by competency, function, and position as opposed to date. Generally, a functional résumé is used for high-level executive positions. A result-focused, chronological résumé is your best choice when applying for a sales position.

Your résumé is a visual representation of you. Gaps in employment are red flags and will be questioned. Format your résumé so it is easy to read. Never have misspelled words or use poor grammar. I have screened out qualified candidates for such mistakes. Despite what you think regarding your job-related experience, or lack thereof, a well-written, well-formatted, results-focused résumé will generate interest and a phone call. It is a mistake to think that experience, education, or clinical background will guarantee an interview. It doesn't matter if you are a seasoned veteran or a beginner trying to break into the industry, your résumé must focus on results.

○ There is no right or wrong way to format a résumé. A chronological résumé is the most common and is best for a sales position. A functional résumé works best for high-level executive positions.

○ Nobody is hired because of a résumé. The sole purpose of a résumé is to generate interest and a phone call.

○ A results-focused résumé will prompt a phone call. Remember, all professional sales positions focus on sales results. The candidate who best communicates sales results via their résumé will generate a phone call and an interview. Your goal is to prompt interest. You want the person reading it to say, "I need to know more about this person."

○ Results should be listed in terms of market share, market share growth, company rank, dollar volume, units sold, forecast attainment, percentage of quota attainment, etc.

o If you do not have sales experience, focus on job-related results from past employment or current employer. Highlight measures applicable to your industry. In other words, focus on results and do not write a job description. Make non-relevant sales experience as relevant as possible to the position you are applying for.

o List all awards and accolades. Support (very briefly) the award with the behavior and result.

o Focus on consistent sales results whenever possible. Managers look for a track record of success. A candidate who delivers results year after year will stand out.

o Focus on relevant results. If you have pharmaceutical, medical device, surgical or biotech sales experience, list your results over time.

o Condense your résumé to two pages whenever possible. It's best if pertinent information can be formatted to fit on a single page, but do not omit results and qualifications for the sole purpose of writing a single-page résumé.

o Do not cram information for the sake of a single-page résumé. Small font and narrow margins are not the answer. Also avoid any visual distraction. Draw the reader to results, not cut and paste quotes, colors, pictures or fancy formatting.

o Never have misspelled words or use poor grammar. Check and recheck. Have your résumé proof read by a professional if possible.

o You are applying for a sales position. Sales people focus on results. Your résumé must do the same. Use the language of results. (*See examples of nouns, modifiers, and action verbs.*)

o Gaps in employment are red flags; avoid them. Be prepared to answer questions regarding any gaps or breaks in employment or education. (*See preparation and face-to-face interviews.*)

o List all education. If you attended a community college, list it. If you transferred, list each school. Missing information and gaps will generate unnecessary questions. These questions simply waste time and may cause the interviewer to doubt. Remember, doubt is the enemy.

o Chronological résumés should include month and year. Listing the year without the month is a yellow flag. Interviewers will ask for specific dates of employment and education.

Example: The XYZ Company, 2004-2008 (yellow flag)
The XYZ Company, May-2004 – September 2008 (preferred)

o Ensure every point on your résumé is accurate and honest. Be prepared to support each point with documentation. Be prepared to discuss every bullet point in detail.

o Ensure your contact information is accurate and up to date.

o Make it easy for people to contact you. Include your cell phone, home phone, and e-mail address.

o Never lie on a résumé! Do not stretch the truth; it will haunt you.

o Use high-quality, neutral-colored paper. Avoid bright colors or fancy formatting. Content and quality will generate interest.

o List references separately. Do not add them to your résumé. Contact your references in advance, ask their permission, and ensure their contact information is accurate. Give two telephone numbers if possible, and know what your references will say when contacted.

o Have your résumé reviewed by a neutral, objective person. Seek that person's opinion and ask for feedback.

o Use a résumé-writing professional, if necessary, who can help with format and content.

o Your résumé should have connectivity and tell a basic story of your education, career, and accomplishments.

o Most organizations only accept résumés electronically. Microsoft Word is the best format because it is widely utilized. Make sure your document opens correctly and is free of glitches. E-mail it to a friend in advance to double check.

o You may have to complete an online questionnaire when you submit your résumé. The questions are generally competency based and are intended to gain insight to your thinking, skills and behavior. Take your time and provide a thorough answer. Use current examples whenever possible. Make sure spelling and grammar are correct before you send.

o You may be asked to complete a job application when you submit a résumé. The same rules apply. Check spelling, grammar and the accuracy of all information before submitting. Most applications will ask current salary and salary desired. Be honest with both. This answer must remain consistent throughout the entire interview process. I have passed on several candidates because they wrote one thing but said another during the interview.

o If you are asked to submit a cover letter with your résumé, ensure it is personalized and specific to the job, not generic.

Briefly state your interest, qualifications and why you are the best candidate. End the letter with a closing statement, "I look forward to meeting with you", "I am available to speak or meet with you at your earliest convenience." There are numerous templates online as reference.

o Use strong language, including action verbs, concrete nouns and positive modifiers.

See examples

Nouns and noun modifiers: Use words such as *ability, actively, competent, consistent, effective, pertinent, proficient, qualified, resourceful, substantially, and versatile.*

This is not an exhaustive list but gives you an idea of the type of language needed to get attention.

Action verbs:

Use words such as *achieved, accomplished, accelerated, administered, analyzed, awarded, conducted, completed, coordinated, created, delegated, demonstrated, designed, developed, directed, earned, evaluated, established, expanded, facilitated, founded, generated, increased, influenced, improved, implemented, initiated, instructed, improved, launched, led, maintained, managed, mastered, motivated, operated, originated, organized, performed, planned, prepared, produced, proposed, proved, provided, proficient in, recommended, reduced, reinforced, reorganized, revamped, revised, reviewed, scheduled, simplified, set up, solved, structured, streamlined, supervised, supported, surpassed, taught, trained, utilized, won and wrote.*

This is not an exhaustive list, but these words will generate interest.

o There are 4 basic questions I ask when I review a résumé:

1. What does the candidate want? (résumé built around the desire to be in pharmaceutical, medical device, surgical or biotech sales)

2. What is he or she qualified to do? (education and employment history)

3. What has the candidate done? (employment history)

4. How well has the candidate done it? (accomplishments, results, and performance)

o Consider the pluses and minuses of your résumé. The person who reviews it will.

A few plus signs at a glance:

+ Success outside of work or school
+ Awards for outstanding achievement and performance
+ Progressive job changes to seek career advancement
+ Pharmaceutical, medical device, surgical or health care-related sales experience
+ Sales volume and/or market share growth
+ Business to business (B2B) sales experience
+ Selling to a similar audience
+ Unique and wide range of activities outside of work or school
+ Broad life experience(s)

A few minus signs at a glance:

- History of leaving sales for non-sales-related jobs
- Years of experience with no clear career progression
- Short time in sales positions and frequent job changes
- Gaps in employment
- Narrative job descriptions
- Lack of results, awards, growth or proven track record of success
- A chronological list of job descriptions

Here is an example of an excellent résumé. I hired this person in 2006, and she is an incredible performer. Notice the language of results and performance.

The name and address have been deleted. Permission was given for this guide.

Jane Ann Doe
123 Main Road, Anytown, MA 01001
Phone (555) 555-5555 E-mail JaneDoe@internet.com

Objective:

Fully utilize my sales, leadership, and training experience with my extensive knowledge in molecular, cellular, developmental biology and practical business skills to achieve top-level performance in the Product Marketing Manager position with XX Pharmaceuticals, Inc. and exceed the annual revenue and contribution targets for XX and all products under my responsibility. As a dynamic, hard working, self-sufficient, enthusiastic, and creative professional with successful consultative sales and project management experience, I will be a powerful and positive addition to the XX sales team. My technical and business background will assist me in promoting XX breakthrough products both internally and externally, allowing me to contribute effectively and directly to the bottom line of XX Pharmaceuticals, Inc.

Education:

University of Colorado, Boulder, Colorado
- Degree: B.S. in Molecular Cellular Developmental Biology, Spring 2004.
- Financed 100% of my education with combination of full-time and part-time work.

Professional Experience:
Territory Manager, *XX Pharmaceuticals, Inc., Boston, MA: 7/2006-present*
- Awarded "Top Gun" during initial New Hire Training in recognition of excellent selling skills, product knowledge, and outstanding attitude
- Achieved "Circle of Excellence" 2007
- Currently ranked 3rd nationally in total bonus payout toward President's Club 2008
- Developed and co-founded Women Ophthalmologists of New England with local and national KOLs XX, MD and XX, MD, including development of a business package pro-bono with Commonwealth Creative Associates advertising agency
- Created the WONE Project Document as a template and guide for other TMs to create their own local ophthalmologist group
- Executed a WONE Free Cataract and Glaucoma Screening at the 2007 AAO in New Orleans with XX, which gained national recognition in Glaucoma News Vol. 6, No. 1
- Assisted with the interview process for the Boston North territory
- Presented the XX PAL program and utilization at GLR POA, January 2008
- Represented XX at multiple local and national industry meetings, including WIO, AAO, and NEOS
- Invited to assist and present at the March 2008 XX New Hire Training
- Invited to participate in XX's first "Marketing Immersion" mini-internship, which included IMS NPA and IPS analysis and development of a sales communication piece to implement the "XX Challenge"

- Grown and maintained relationships with local, regional, national, and international KOLs including XX, YY, TT, RR, SS, HH, and MM

Sales Representative, District Trainer, *XXX XXX Pharmaceutical, Denver, CO: 5/2005-7/2006*
- Ranked 1st in product growth in the nation for a fenofibrate
- Ranked 2nd in sales in the Western Region among 62 sales representatives for a statin
- Promoted to District Trainer and provided Phase II home-office new hire training
- Coached and mentored district members in a ride-along setting
- Selected as Innovation panel delegate and contributor
- Led one new product launch and reintroduced two additional products to my market

Sales Consultant, *Mountain States Motors, Denver, CO: 7/2004-5/2005 (full-time, commission only)*
- Sales of new and pre-owned automobiles for large automotive dealership
- Sold third top volume in the first month
- Achieved top salesperson in the third month of my employment
- Consistently one of the top three salespersons since beginning of employment (and consistently was the highest profit-generating salesperson across two dealerships among 27 salespeople)

Supervisor, Telephone Outreach Program, *CU Foundation, Boulder, CO: 2002-2003 (part-time)*
- Managed a team of 25 Telephone Associates.
- Coached and mentored 15 assigned Telephone Associates.

- Developed and implemented processes to improve the overall effectiveness of Telephone Outreach Program.

Telephone Associate – Telephone Outreach Program, *CU Foundation, Boulder, CO: 2001 (part-time)*
- Achieved my goal of raising over $10,000 for the University of Colorado academic programs

Academic and Extracurricular Activities:
- Harvard Cataract Intensive Course at Massachusetts Eye and Ear Infirmary
- Ocular Immunology and Uveitis Foundation–Walk For Vision 2006 and 2007
- Massachusetts Eye Research and Surgery Institute Physician Education Conference 2006 and 2007
- Women Ophthalmologists of New England
- Ophthalmic Women Leaders
- National Society for Collegiate Scholars –University of Colorado
- Chemistry Club–University of Colorado
- Rotarian Leadership Conference–Estes Park, Colorado
- Rotarian Scholarship award
- Wells Fargo Bank Scholarship award
- CTRC Volunteer–worked with disabled children in weekly physical therapy sessions

Personal:
- Trained and accomplished Public Speaker
- Raised over $6,000 and completed the three-day, 60-mile Avon Breast Cancer Charity Walk
- PADI certified
- Ran in the Harpoon Brewery 5-Miler Race 2008 to benefit the Angel Fund

A note for medical device and surgical candidates: Due to the transactional nature and highly competitive environment of medical device sales, organizations and hiring managers demand a results-oriented candidate. Device sales are the most lucrative in the industry, which is why it is so competitive. Medical device companies screen out more than 95 percent of applicants during the résumé review. In fact, many device companies will not interview or hire pharmaceutical sales representatives because they feel they are not "real" sales people. Pharmaceutical sales are promotional as opposed to transactional. There is a very distinct difference. It is critical to "hyper-focus" your résumé on any transactional selling experience. If you have business-to-business (B2B) experience, let that be the highlight of your résumé. Of course, your results must remain the focus.

For those of you with an advanced degree such as an MBA, Nursing Degree, Pharm D, etc. it is critical for you to focus on results as well. Your clinical experience should be noted but the focus must remain on performance. Be prepared to answer questions pertaining to your degree. What made you decide to pursue that field, what have you done with your degree, why sales, how will you utilize your education to increase sales results just to name a few.

There are numerous guides, books, resources, and websites on the art of résumé writing. Most of them will give you similar advice on formatting, language, and structure. The biggest mistake people make is assuming their vast experience in pharmaceuticals or health care will generate a phone call. It will not. Review your résumé with a critical eye. Take a "what's wrong with it" point of view to help you identify any areas that need attention. Use objective third-party professionals to scour through and identify questionable information. If you were the interviewer or person screening your résumé, what would you ask? What would impress you? What would prompt you to want to find out more? Why would your résumé cause someone to pick up the phone and call you? Will your résumé sit on the bottom or top of the stack of one hundred fifty others?

"By failing to prepare, you are preparing to fail."

- Benjamin Franklin

PREPARATION: THE KEY
TO INTERVIEW SUCCESS

Preparation does not guarantee an interview. Preparation does not guarantee a job offer. However, *lack of preparation does guarantee you will achieve neither.* It is the number one reason I do not hire particular candidates. Why would I hire someone who did not take the time to prepare? I expect people to take time and be ready for their interview. People who do not prepare stand out for all the wrong reasons. I call it "negative attention." There is no excuse for not being prepared for an interview. It is cliché, but you only get one chance to make a first impression. Preparedness speaks to resourcefulness, interest, organization, commitment, and time management. These are the same competencies of good salespeople. Preparation is the single most important aspect of the hiring process. Do not rush or cram. Take the time to thoroughly prepare for each interview. Network with family and friends, and use all resources (not just the Internet) to help you prepare. If you want the position, it is necessary—not suggested—that you prepare and practice throughout the process. Remember, you are preparing for a professional sales position. The entire process involves selling yourself to the employer. Think of the employer as the buyer of a product and that product is you. Are you the best product the employer can purchase? Preparation and readiness is the key.

As I've said, pharmaceutical, medical device, surgical and biotech sales are lucrative but extremely competitive. The field is packed with qualified and experienced candidates. Unfortunately, experience alone will not guarantee an interview or a position. Those who take the time to prepare improve their chances dramatically. Most candidates do not present their skills effectively. Why? Lack of preparation of course. It is estimated nearly 90 percent of candidates cannot effectively communicate the skills and behaviors they possess to support their ability to do the job. That is a sad commentary. Pharmaceutical and health care organizations are professional and demanding. They expect candidates to be highly organized and prepared to meet the rigorous demands of the job.

○ Come to the interview prepared! This is the most important and basic action you can take. It is also one of the few things you control during the process. You will not fool the person interviewing if you are not prepared. Common questions asked during an interview are intended to "weed out" a candidate's level of preparation. I have cut interviews short due to lack of readiness. I will not waste my time with a person who did not invest the time to prepare for an interview.

○ Research the company through the Internet, but please do more. Talk to colleagues, doctors and pharmacists; go to the library; network with friends and family. This is an excellent way to show the interviewer how resourceful you are and the commitment you have for the position and the organization. Many times I will ask, "How did you conduct research?" The candidate who is well prepared, organized, and resourceful always gets my attention.

o Conduct a background check on the company. Background information should include company history, competition, culture, size, earnings, Wall Street performance, executive management team, business model, products, pipeline, mission statement, and value propositions. Do your home-work, using the Internet, library, newspaper, journals, and personal networking. Remember, there is more to research than the Internet.

> **Common research websites are:**
> www.corporateinformation.com
> www.news.google.com
> www.news.yahoo.com
> www.hoovers.com

o Conduct market research on the territory, including com-petitive environment, managed care landscape, local hos-pitals, and pharmacies. Use the Internet to research infor-mation. Visit local hospitals, pharmacies, and physician offices. Be creative; be resourceful.

o Make a research checklist. Set goals and list what you want to accomplish each day. It is extra work but well worth it.

_____

o Print pertinent, job-specific information. Bring it to the interview in a binder or folder. Again, this demonstrates great interest, resourcefulness and your ability to gather critical information. There are hundreds of websites you can search to gather local information on the territory and products.

o Note any information of interest about the company, products, or territory. This knowledge will be of value during the face-to-face interview. Your ability to conduct in-depth research demonstrates a high level of interest, an eye for detail, and your commitment to the job. Most candidates fall short in this category. You will stand out among your competition.

o Know the products you will be selling and research them. Know the basic information as well as the main competitors. You should also know the correct pronunciation of each product. You do not have to be a product expert, but take the initiative to learn as much as possible about the products you will be selling. Pharmaceutical and medical sales are technical. Take the time to learn the basics of the product, the disease they treat and the utility of the medical or surgical device you may be selling.

o Obtain sales and marketing pieces if possible. Quite often doctors' offices have copies. Visit an office and ask the staff if you can have them. Marketing materials will give you insight into the product and the company's image. This is especially useful if you are trying to break into the industry. If you are trying to separate yourself from another candidate, this will do it. Some managers will ask you to role play during the interview. Having the marketing materials in advance will give you a competitive advantage. Make sure to review them prior to your interview.

o Create a professional brag book. (Use a presentation folder, organized and labeled.)

o Include up-to-date résumé, copies of several field contact/coaching reports, several past performance reviews, a list of references, history of performance (sales, market share, rankings, etc.), significant accomplishments and rewards, and any job or competency-related information that demonstrates transferable skill and ability. Include customer recommendation letters as well. Your brag book is not *War and Peace*. Keep it concise, job related, relevant, progressive, and results focused. Use online references and templates if necessary. It should tell a basic story of your career.

○ **Create a one-minute summary on why you are changing jobs or looking for a new job.** You will be asked this question at every interview. Do not get trapped by over speaking this answer. Avoid a long-winded confession. Do not create doubt in the mind of the interviewer.

\
\
\
\
\
\
\
\
\
\
\
\
\

○ **Create a one-minute summary on why you are the best person for the job.** Be confident as you summarize the results you will deliver. Include job competencies, skills, and behaviors you will demonstrate to be successful.

```
_____
_____
_____
_____
_____
_____
_____
_____
_____
_____
_____
_____
_____
```

o Prepare and practice how you will ask for the job. How will you ask what the next steps are in the interview process? This is an expectation not a suggestion.

_____

_____

_____

_____

_____

_____

_____

_____

_____

_____

_____

_____

_____

o Create a 30-60-90 day plan or basic business plan. (Use a presentation folder.) Include product education, territory logistics and call plan, key customers, managed care, manager expectations, and results expected. Be prepared to discuss how you will execute your plan and increase market share and sales as a result. If you have never written a 30-60-90 plan, conduct a Google or Yahoo search for suggestions and templates. The basic format will be provided, but it's up to you to make it job specific and results-oriented. In other words, make it your plan.

o Write a list (be specific) as to why you are the best candidate for the job. Focus on job-pertinent qualities, skills, and behaviors. Reference the first chapter, "What Are We Looking For?" Identify transferable skills, abilities, and results.

_____
_____
_____
_____
_____
_____
_____
_____
_____
_____
_____
_____
_____
_____

o Print the job description from the company website or job posting. This will give you tremendous insight into the exact competencies, skills, and behaviors they are looking for. Expectations of the candidate are generally listed. Be prepared to discuss each throughout the interview. Your goal is to communicate how and why you match the company's description of the "ideal" candidate. Prepare yourself as the ideal candidate; sell yourself as the ideal candidate.

o If there is no job description on the website, call the company and request one. Human resources departments will e-mail a sales job description to you if one is not available on the company website. If the company is unwilling to e-mail one, ask for the qualifications and expectations of the job verbally. Note the key competencies.

o Make a test run to the interview location if necessary. Assume nothing; do not trust MapQuest or your GPS. Getting lost is an unacceptable excuse for being late. Actually, there is almost *no* excuse for being late.

o If you are flying to an interview, check your flight in advance. Always have the airline or travel agents telephone number programed in your phone in case there are last minute changes. If you are delayed, it's best to call the interviewer and let them know. An e-mail may or may not get to them. Do not check a bag with your interview materials. Carry on whenever possible. Use your time in the air for final preparation.

o Prepare everything well in advance of the interview. Do not cram the morning of or the night before. Be well rested in advance of any interview.

o Research the people who are interviewing you. A Google or Yahoo search of the interviewer's name may provide insight. You may find useful information on LinkedIn. Use this information throughout the interview when appropriate.

o Remember, you are getting ready for a sales interview. Be prepared to sell yourself, your qualifications, and your results every step of the way. Don't be prideful or boastful but confident of the skills, abilities, and results you will deliver.

o Bring a copy of your W-2 tax form from the previous year(s) in case you are asked to prove salary. This has become common practice.

o Research the disease states of the products you will be selling. Be prepared to discuss at a basic level. Surgical and medical device candidates should have a basic idea of the equipment or device, where and how it is used, and the competitive environment.

o Practice pronunciation of products. If you don't know, find out. A local pharmacy can offer assistance.

o E-mail the interviewer prior to the interview. Say that you are looking forward to the meeting and thank the interviewer for his or her time. This will set you apart from most.

o Bring multiple copies of your résumé, brag book and anything you want to leave behind. Print everything on the same type of paper—no copies, all originals whenever possible

o If you are asked to fill out paperwork or an application prior to the interview, complete it prior to the interview. I have seen many candidates filling out paperwork while they're waiting. This makes me wonder if the candidate is a procrastinator.

o Prepare questions, and write or print them in advance.

o Many interviews begin late. No worries; use the time to review your questions and mentally prepare.

o Check then double check the exact location and time of the interview.

o If working with a recruiter, spend as much time as possible researching and gaining insight into the company and people. Recruiters will most often be your best resource. Listen and heed their advice.

o Expect the unexpected. There may be more than one person interviewing, or you could interview in front of a panel.

The company may want to conduct a second interview that same day. Many times, two managers will interview together. They may invite a sales trainer or sales representative to assist as well. This is a common practice in pharmaceutical, biotech, and medical sales interviews.

o Be prepared for a fifteen-, thirty-, sixty- or ninety-minute interview. There are no rules. I have interviewed people for 2½ hours when they were expecting a forty-five-minute interview.

o Identify the competencies or value propositions of the company you are interviewing with. Generally, the company website is your best resource. Print it, learn it, and carry it with you.

o If you know people in the organization you are interviewing with, call or meet with them to gather as much pertinent information as possible. Who better to provide insight than current employees? A word of caution: be careful not to make assumptions based on what an employee may say about their employer.

o Prepare for the interview much like you would before an important presentation. Role-play and rehearse answers, questions, and points on your résumé.

o Write down your answers to some of the common questions. This is extra work but well worth it. (*See Sample Questions.*)

o Think of, write down, and practice the specific situations, actions, and results you will use when asked behavioral questions. *STAR* is an excellent method to remember: *Situation, Task, Action, and Result.* Your examples should be relevant, recent, and specific to the position. Use multiple examples and situations to demonstrate depth. This action is a must do! (*See Behavioral Interviews & Targeted Selection.*)

o If you are trying to break into the industry, have a good reason(s) why you have chosen this field. Make it real; make it honest. Avoid clichés such as "I am a people person" or "It's been my lifelong dream to get into medical sales."

o Be prepared to discuss the details of your current bonus structure. Know your market share, share growth, percent attainment, and rank within the district, region, and nation. Discuss how you were measured and what the expectations were. I am always concerned when a candidate cannot explain his or her current bonus program or does not know any of the above information. "I just work hard and let the bonus take care of itself." I have eliminated candidates for such answers. This applies to all candidates with sales experience regardless of industry.

o Know every point on your résumé, every proof source, every date, every time line, every award, and every responsibility. Can you to discuss in detail when asked? Make sure you are ready.

o Write and practice telling "your story." If asked, "Tell me about yourself," you will be ready. Your story should be narrative but concise, job/business related and have a fluid feel. Interviewers are looking for connectivity, judgment, honesty, and consistency.

---

o Communication and professionalism are two underlying competencies or behaviors interviewers assess throughout the interview process. Practice your answers as if you were practicing a sales presentation. You need to communicate clearly and professionally.

o Practice body language and eye contact. Also, practice the pace of your answers as well as tone. Role-play and rehearse in front of a mirror if necessary. If you are interviewing in the morning, have a conversation with someone (anyone) before the meeting. Do not let the interview be the first conversation of the day. Consider it a warm-up exercise for your brain.

o Answer all the questions listed in this guide, and rehearse them as if it was your actual interview. You can also find hundreds of other questions on the Internet or at the library. You should not be surprised by any question asked. We live in the information age. If you have a friend, colleague, or family member in the industry, ask them what types of questions are asked. When you are prepared, you are not surprised.

o Send a thank-you card or an e-mail to any person who helped you in your preparation. The health care industry is all about networking. Opportunities arise when least expected. You want to be the person they remember and will help again.

The curse of too...
- *Too comfortable, too fast*
- *Too confident*
- *Too wordy*
- *Too general*
- *Too emotional*

- *Too intense*
- *Too inconsistent*
- *Too indecisive*
- *Too relaxed*
- *Too rigid*
- *Too quirky*
- *Too confident*
- *Too unprepared*
- *Too many questions*
- *Too desperate*

There are many more. Are you too___? Self-reflect and make the necessary adjustments. You do not want the interviewer to say, "The candidate was too (fill in the blank) after you're gone. Remember, **doubt is the enemy**. Doubt will separate one candidate from the next in the mind of the hiring manager. **Preparation is the key to confidence**. I have no doubt; this guide will prepare you for interview success!

"Success is the sum of small efforts,
repeated day in and day out."

—*Robert Collier*

SECRETS TO A SUCCESSFUL
PHONE SCREEN

I believe the phone screen is the most underestimated part of the hiring process. Human resources managers and sales managers are trained to conduct phone screens. Basically, we are looking for people to screen in rather than screen out. Unfortunately, we screen more candidates out than we screen in. The process begins with your results-focused résumé.

Your résumé created interest and generated the phone call. Congratulations, mission accomplished. Now prepare for the phone screen much like you would prepare for a face-to face interview. The questions you ask and the passion you exhibit on the phone are extremely important. Obviously, the person conducting the phone screen cannot read your body language. However, the screener will make judgments and assessments through the tone of your voice and your preparedness during the call. Phone screeners take copious notes. Be accurate and honest with every answer. Be especially precise with timelines regarding education and employment as well as salaries and bonus. Do not hedge on any answer. If you are unsure of a specific, tell the person you will get back to him or her with the exact information. You must speak in absolutes, not generalities.

If you make it to the face-to-face interview, the hiring manager should have the notes from the phone screen and will ask similar questions, looking for consistency in your answers. The smallest discrepancy can create doubt and may mean the difference between success and failure.

It is not only appropriate but expected that you ask for a face-to-face interview. Remember, you are interviewing for a sales position. As in any sale, asking for the business is required. Without being overanxious or too aggressive, ask for the interview.

One last note: Make sure the greeting on your answering machine and voice mail are professional. Singing, music or kids are cute but not professional. Whether you agree or disagree, it sends a message to the person calling, a message that may not be positive.

- The biggest mistake candidates make is underestimating the importance of a phone screen. It is your first person-to-person interaction. Be prepared and confident.

- Conduct your phone screen in a quiet place, away from noise and distraction. Please, no Starbucks.

- Make every effort to conduct the phone screen as soon as possible. Time is the enemy. A delay may be a missed opportunity.

- Eliminate any chance of being interrupted.

- Never conduct a phone screen while driving.

- If you are new to the industry, spend time in the field and meet with potential customers prior to the interview. Network with family and friends. Be resourceful.

o Generally phone screens are designed to screen in candidates not screen out candidates. Your only goal is to secure a face-to-face interview.

o Phone screens will identify yellow- and red-flag hiring issues: high salary, low energy, lack of experience, organizational fit, motivation, past performance, etc.

o Be 100 percent honest and accurate regarding education, employment history, dates of employment, and salary. In fact, be 100 percent honest with every detail.

o Know the reason why you want to leave your current organization and why you are interested in the available position. Your answer should be no longer than a minute. This question is guaranteed. Rehearse your answer in advance.

o Know every point on your résumé and be prepared to discuss each. The phone screener will be referencing it extensively during the call.

o Prepare questions in advance of the call. The job may not be the right fit for you. Asking the right questions will prevent you and the employer from wasting time. Plus the questions you ask will prove to be useful during the face-to-face interview.

o Is there a time of day when mentally you are at your best (i.e. "I'm a morning person.")? If so, try to arrange your phone screen to coincide.

o Ask the person conducting the phone screen his or her name and role in the company. Make note on a piece of paper for future reference. You may be able to make reference during the face-to-face interview. This is an excellent habit to establish during every step of the interview process.

45

o If calling from a cell phone, make sure you have a good signal and battery life. Get the interviewer's direct number in case you are disconnected. Tell the person you will call back immediately if that happens.

o Have a pen and paper available during your phone screen in case you need to take notes, jot down a phone number or interview location, etc.

o Phone screens are not "confessionals." Avoid dissertations, long-winded answers and too much information about your personal life. In fact, avoid dissertations on any question.

o This may sound strange, but don't let the phone screen be your first conversation of the day. In other words, have interaction and conversation with somebody prior to the call. Consider it a "warm-up" conversation.

o There is almost *no* excuse for making the interviewer arrange his or her schedule to fit yours. Remember, it's about the interviewer not you.

o Obtain the e-mail address of the phone screener, and follow-up with a thank-you note within 24 hours or the same day if possible.

o Close and ask for a face-to-face interview. Be ambitious, positive, confident, and motivated. Make yourself available for the interview as soon as possible.

o Review each question in this interview guide. Rehearse your answers. You know we are looking for. There should be no surprise question. Interviews conducted over the phone are no different than those in person, and the objective is the same.

"A wise man will make more opportunities than he finds."

—*Francis Bacon*

FACE-TO-FACE INTERVIEWS

Congratulations, you have made it to the face-to-face interview. This is your chance to sell yourself to the hiring manager(s). You have prepared for this opportunity and have earned the right to sit face-to-face with your future employer. Take it seriously and practice, practice, practice before the interview. Remember, you are interviewing for a professional sales position. You must sell your qualifications, skills, and ability to deliver sales results to every person you are interviewing with. Do not assume the interviewer knows how good you are from reading your résumé. Your résumé created interest and generated a phone call. Now you must sell your qualifications. It's also a mistake to think you are the best-qualified candidate because of your vast experience or clinical background. Often, years of experience are a disadvantage. You must communicate your ability to transfer your skills and abilities to the new organization. I hire people who are confident in their ability to deliver consistent sales results. If you are trying to break into the industry, you must demonstrate behaviors and skills from your previous experiences that will transfer to pharmaceutical, medical device, surgical or biotech sales. No matter how qualified you are, do not underestimate your competition. There is always someone with more experience, better qualifications, and superior sales results. Never are two candidates equal.

The goal of a first interview is to secure a second and third interview if necessary. You must bring your "A" game and be the best you can be. It is cliché, but you only get one chance to make a first impression. Remember, communication and professionalism is being evaluated from the moment you shake the person's hand at introduction until the time you ask for the job. Apply the best practices, but more importantly, avoid the pitfalls. The difference between you and the next candidate may be miniscule. Treat the interview as the single most important aspect of the hiring process because it is.

o The hiring manager's objective during a first face-to-face interview is to determine three things: Does the candidate qualify for a second interview? Do I want to learn more? Does the candidate fit?

o Generally the first interview is a "fit and feel" interview. Does the interviewer feel good about the person? Does he or she want to dig deeper and learn more about this candidate? Will the candidate fit into the organization and the team? Rarely does an organization make a hiring decision from a single interview.

o During the first interview, the interviewer will ask questions about previous employment and education. Many times a first interview is a screening interview. This is especially true if there was not a formal phone screen. Information gathered determine areas that need further exploration on the second interview.

o The interviewer is always assessing the candidate's skills, abilities and behaviors. Will they transfer to the new position?

o The second interview is the "telling" interview. In other words, the second interview determines the best candidate and the runner-up candidate. There is always a best candidate; never are two candidates equal. Your main goal is to be invited back for a second interview.

o When in doubt, check it out. If a hiring manager is unsure of a candidate based on the first interview, he or she generally will invite the person back for a second. Some people simply do not do well on their first interview even though they are very qualified. We are trained to check it out when there is doubt. The second interview will focus on any area of doubt. It may be a skill, past experience, sales result, a point on your résumé, etc.

o You will know that an interviewer has doubt if you are asked repeated questions on the same topic or if the interviewer spends an inordinate amount of time on one area. Recognize this, and confidently and concisely address any doubt and concern.

o Arrive early. Greet any staff (hotel/restaurant) with professionalism. Quite often, interviewers will ask a front desk person or staff member for feedback on his or her initial impression of each candidate.

o Be 100 percent truthful about your current salary and bonus. Do not guess or estimate what your salary is. Also, do not hedge when asked. Find out prior to the interview.

o Be 100 percent truthful in every answer. Interviewers are trained to uncover dishonesty. Body language conveys honesty and dishonesty. Confidence is king. When you are confident and truthful, it shows. The opposite is also true.

o It is important to tell your future employer why you want the job—why you want to join the organization as opposed to why you want to leave your current employer. I want to hire someone who wants to work for my company not someone who wants to leave theirs. Avoid long-winded dissertations on how bad your current employer is. Avoid long-winded dissertations on any topic. Do not let your message get lost in the words.

o Exhibit positive, confident body language, and avoid quirky or nervous habits. Be attentive, polite, and professional. Demonstrate positive self-awareness.

o Control your tone and pace. Make adjustments suitable to the interviewing environment.

o Visualize yourself as a member of the organization. This will help connect with the interviewer who is trying to identify the best job fit. Job fit is a critical piece in the hiring puzzle, and it is rather subjective. Connectivity is extremely important.

o Prepare your questions in advance. Write or type them, but have them organized and easily accessible. Every candidate asks about training. While this is not a bad question, ask more in-depth questions. Ask about business model, the future of the company, the culture, the background of the interviewers. What are the expectations, what does the ideal candidate possess, what are the characteristics of the company's most successful sales people, and what are the challenges and greatest opportunities of the territory? The list goes on.

o Do not wear strong-scented perfumes or colognes. They can distract, and many people have allergies to fragrances.

o Dress professionally as if you were going to work in the field that day. Avoid flashy dress, loud ties and bold jewelry. It's not a party or a wedding; it's an interview. Men: shoes polished, buttons buttoned, shirts ironed, suits pressed, ties at the "right" length, all belt loops used, hair and face groomed and please, no cufflinks. Ladies: business suits pressed, hair and outer appearance groomed, and please, keep the sunglasses off your head, your spiked heels and crazy handbags in the closet, and the amount of skin you show in check!

o Be prepared to role-play a product you currently sell or one of the products you will be selling. An interviewer may give you a sales piece and ask you to role-play on the spot.

o Speak the language of a salesperson. Remember, you are interviewing for a professional sales position. The primary role is to sell, not educate. *Pre-call planning, opening, probing, supporting, closing, and post-call analysis* are the words of a professional salesperson.

o Be prepared to discuss each point of your résumé in a concise, results-oriented manner. Communicate applicability to the position you are interviewing for. This is especially important for those without prior medical or pharmaceutical sales experience.

o Make appropriate eye contact, but don't overdo it. Too much direct eye contact can make the interviewer uncomfortable.

o Be mindful of your body language. Studies have shown that of the information that we receive from other people: **10%** is from what they actually say; **40%** is from the tone and speed of their voice; **50%** is from their body language.

Head

- *A tilted head symbolizes interest in someone or something.*
- *A lowered head is a negative signal that communicates acceptance of defeat.*
- *Fondling or patting down hair demonstrates insecurity and a lack of self-confidence.*
- *The occasional nod from a listener to a speaker is a positive message; it's an indication that they are listening and are interested.*
- *Too much nodding implies that a listener has lost interest, is not really listening and is simply nodding to be polite.*
- *A person stroking their chin is evaluating or making a decision.*
- *Projecting the chin towards another person demonstrates defiance or aggression.*
- *Clearing the throat or swallowing air is a sign of anxiety.*

Eyes

- *Failing to look someone in the eyes displays a lack of confidence.*
- *Lowering the eyes is a sign of submission, fear or guilt.*
- *Staring is interpreted as aggression and implies a person feels dominant and powerful.*
- *Looking directly into another person's eyes without staring signifies self-assurance.*
- *Blink rate increases when someone is nervous or assessing something.*
- *Looking upwards and to the right indicates that someone is recalling a memory.*
- *Looking upwards and to the left implies that a person is using the imaginative / creative part of their brain.*
- *When a person looks directly upwards they are thinking.*
- *People who feel insulted, caught-out or threatened, will likely break eye contact.*
- *A quick glance sideways during a conversation can be used to show irritation at the last comment made.*

- *A person who consistently looks around them is bored with a situation / conversation.*

Upper Body

- *A person with folded or crossed arms is placing a barrier between themselves and their surroundings; indicating that they're not happy with what is being said or done.*
- *Open arms; mean that someone is approachable and willing to communicate with others.*
- *Outward, upward hand movements express an open and positive message.*
- *Positioning hands behind the back shows that someone is relaxed and comfortable; though it can also be used on purpose to convey a message of power and confidence.*
- *Finger pointing is interpreted as either a sign of assertiveness or a sign of aggression.*
- *Tapping or drumming fingers communicates impatience or frustration.*
- *Fiddling with items (e.g. keys or a pen) can be a sign of nerves or anxiety; alternatively it may be done as a result of boredom or impatience.*

o Bring several clean copies of your résumé, reference letters, and brag book. You never know how many people will show up to interview. Make sure you have a copy for each.

o Stand until asked or told where to sit.

o Take a personal day or vacation day from your current employer. Many interviewers will ask how you are accounting for your time out of the field while interviewing. Take "official" time off and be honest. If you flinch, you're in trouble.

o Know your strengths. One of the most common interview questions is "What are your strengths?" Bullet point and give a brief commentary. Do not become too narrative in your answers. Relate your strengths to the position you are applying for.

_____

_____

_____

_____

_____

_____

_____

o Know your weaknesses. The second most common question is "What is your area of development or opportunity?" This question will reveal the candidate's level of self-awareness. It's not a bad thing to admit you have areas of development. Identify them, and inform the interviewer what you have done or are doing to improve.

_____

_____

_____

_____

_____

_____

_____

o Focus on results orientation. Avoid abstracts, philosophy, long narratives, and assumptions. Focus your answer on your ability to deliver sales results. Provide real examples of how you have done this in past roles.

"This is how I will grow sales...Let me give you examples of how."

"This is how I grew sales in my previous organization...May I share my results with you?"

"This is what I will deliver to the organization...I have a track record of performance; let me tell you the steps I'll take to deliver outstanding results."

o Remain focused on sales, growing sales, growing market share and exceeding quota. Remember, these are the priorities of a salesperson. Activity is important, but activity in order to deliver sales results is the key. Working hard and being busy only matter when they yield a result.

o Be a positive person. I want to hire someone with a positive attitude.

o Harsh, but true: What's right with you? What's wrong with you? Can I spend eight hours in the car with this person? What problems or limitations might you bring to the job? These are the basic thoughts of an interviewer. The interviewer may not ask it but is thinking it, so prepare for it.

o Be concise. Many times, less is more. Your painstaking preparation should have included practicing your answers in a concise manner.

o When asked what motivates you, it's okay to be motivated by money; after all, this is a sales position. Don't sound apologetic. People pursue sales positions to make money.

o Many interviewers will use humor in an effort to have the candidate "drop his or her guard." This is an interviewing tactic. Do not get trapped by feeling too comfortable too quickly. Follow the tips and suggestions in this guide regardless of whether you think the interviewer likes you or not.

o Speak of ability not of need. Remember, it's not about you; it's about them. In other words, do not communicate desperation. Remain focused on your ability to deliver the sales results they desire. You want the company to need you more than you need it.

o Please avoid answering "I can't remember" when asked résumé related questions. You should know every point on your résumé and be able to discuss in detail.

o Remember this management premise: Past performance predicts future behavior. Focus on consistent ability to deliver results over time.

o Have a well-prepared and honest answer when asked, "Why are you looking for another position?" Your answer must be honest, concise, confident, and about one minute long. Rehearse your answer in advance.

o Use a pen as a pointer when referencing an area of your résumé or brag book. This demonstrates ability to highlight information using a visual aid. Professional salespeople use visual aids as reference. An interview is a sales presentation. The product is you.

o Silence is golden. Do not over speak the interview, and do not speak when there are no questions being asked. A skilled interviewer will be silent as a test to see if the candidate can also remain quiet. Remember, a good salesperson is an excellent listener.

o Do not wear your emotions on your sleeve. In other words, an interview is not an opportunity to confess your past and disclose information that has no bearing on the present job. If discussing your past elicits an emotional response, redirect the question to focus on the present and future. I have interviewed candidates who became emotional during the interview and found it extremely difficult to move forward.

o Do not treat the interview like a confessional. Too much information will distract from facts that are pertinent to the present job. Divulging information will generate additional questions that may not be job related. You may create doubt regarding your character and judgment in the mind of the interviewer. Doubt is the enemy during the interview process.

o Be confident and bold but not arrogant or cocky. Remember you are an invited candidate, show gratitude and appreciation.

o Be ready for the question "What separates you from the rest of the pack? Why you?" Your diligent preparation has paved the way for this question.

o Salary questions and financial expectations will be discussed, so be prepared. You may answer, "My focus is finding the right opportunity just as you are looking to find the right candidate. I will be open to any fair offer." The important point is to answer with confidence that you are the right person for the position. You may be asked for a salary range, so to have your number(s) ready in advance.

o Write down or repeat the names of those you are interviewing with so you don't forget. Identify their roles in the company if they don't tell you at the beginning of the interview. You want to know who is asking questions.

o If you want to take notes, ask for permission.

o Interviewers take copious notes. Do not be distracted by the appearance that they may not be listening.

o If the interviewer is quietly taking notes, avoid filling the silence with chatter.

o Be an intense listener. If you need clarity or do not understand the question, ask for it to be repeated rather than guess.

o Ask the manager what is expected of the person being hired.

o Be clear and confident regarding your career goals. You don't need to know exactly what you want to do every year for your entire career, but have a good idea of the direction in which you want to go and why. Managers look for connectivity in this answer. In other words, do your career goals match your résumé?

o Do not answer questions that are not asked. Take advice from attorneys: They never prove what they do not need to prove.

o You are not in control of the interview. Do not take charge. If you feel like you are talking too much, you probably are. If the interviewer is struggling to ask questions, you're talking too much. Read the body language of the interviewer. I can't emphasize this point enough. Be mindful of how much you are speaking!

o Use the word "I," not "we" or "us." You want the results to be yours and yours alone. The word "I" demonstrates personal ownership and accountability. "We" and "us" communicate a transfer of ownership. Selling yourself is the purpose of the interview. "We" and "us" may create doubt in the mind of the interviewer. This is especially true for pharmaceutical representatives who may have worked in a "POD" or "cluster" setting.

o Do not get caught discussing your age or personal matters.

o Try to avoid clichés, such as "I'm a people person."

o Medical device and surgical candidates: Be prepared to discuss the quality of your selling skills. Provide examples of customer interactions, buy and bill, and the transactional sales process.

o Read the body language of the interviewer, especially when the interview is coming to a close. Do not become overanxious or over-talkative because the interview is coming to a close. Set the tone, be confident, and ask if there are any remaining questions.

o Questions you may want to ask:
   Why is the position open?
   What are your expectations?
   Tell me about your bonus program?
   What resources do your representatives have?
   What do you think the future of the organization is?
   What is your background, and what brought you to the company?
   How would you describe your leadership or management style?
   What traits describe your most successful salespeople?
   What does the ideal candidate look like?

o Interviewers take note of thought-provoking questions. Your research should have prompted several in-depth questions. Lackluster questions may cost you the job.

o **Ask for the job** or to be considered for the next step. This is a professional sales position. Closing is an expectation not an option.

o Ask what the next step is, when a decision will be made, and when you can expect to hear from them.

o Ask to spend a day in the field with an existing sales representative.

o Ask how the company will communicate its decision or if you need to follow up.

o Ask if the interviewer has any remaining questions, or if you need to provide any additional information. If so, follow up immediately.

o Leave behind your brag book, 30-60-90 or basic business plan, overview of the territory and the results you anticipate delivering. Offer a copy to each person.

o Ask the people you meet with for their business cards. Send a thank-you note to every person immediately following the interview. An e-mail is perfectly acceptable. Make sure it is short and sweet. A very brief summary of why you are the best candidate is also appropriate.

"Thinking is easy, acting is difficult, and to put one's thoughts into action is the most difficult thing in the world."

—*Johann Wolfgang von Goethe*

BEHAVIORAL INTERVIEWS
TARGETED SELECTION®

You hear the term, but what does it mean? The behavioral interview, often referred to as Targeted Selection®, is the most common method used to hire salespeople in the pharmaceutical, medical, surgical and biotech industry. Why? Because it works. A behavioral interview is competency based, designed to identify specific skills, abilities, and behaviors. The behavioral interview is founded on the premise that past performance predicts future behavior. The goal of every behavioral interview is to collect specific job-related skills, behaviors, and real-life experiences from candidates, regardless of their current employer and previous work history. Behavioral interviews focus on facts and actual situations. They are objective, not subjective, and are designed to take emotion out of the decision. As a candidate, you want a behavioral interview because it is fair, objective, and founded on job-specific criteria.

Organizations that utilize behavioral interviewing as their primary method of hiring generally develop a list of six to eight competencies. The competencies they choose are the specific behaviors needed in order for a person to be successful in that position. Human resources departments and sales management determine the "core" competencies necessary for each position. For example, results orientation and the ability to overcome obstacles are always core competencies for a professional sales position. Many job postings list the competencies for the ideal candidate. Print the job description and identify the job competencies. Interview questions will focus on these specific behaviors. There is no need to be surprised.

To be successful you must be able to identify a behavioral question, then provide a specific example related to the competency. Earlier, I mentioned the term STAR, which stands for **S**ituation, **T**ask, **A**ction, and **R**esult. The interviewer is evaluating your ability to provide a specific situation, your task in that situation, the actions you took, and finally, the result you achieved. They want specific examples, actions, and results from your past in an attempt to predict the future. For those already in pharmaceutical or medical sales, your STAR examples need to be current and relevant. For those trying to break in, examples need to be transferable and adaptive. Finally, for those interviewing for medical device or surgical sales, your examples must be transactional in nature. There should be a direct cause and effect. In other words, your actions resulted in sales. I have included many examples in this guide. In every answer to every behavioral question, be specific and provide a result.

Interviewers are trained to focus on five basic interview principles:

1. Use past behavior to predict future behavior. Behavior in one situation usually predicts behavior in a similar situation at a later time.

2. Interview for the critical job requirements. The interviewer is guided by a list of skills, special qualities,

knowledge, or behavior for the position he or she is interviewing for. The list is developed by identifying those aspects of on-the-job performance that are most critical to getting the job done.

3. Base hiring decisions on the evaluation of applicant information accumulated from a variety of sources.

4. Apply effective interviewing skills and techniques. Follow the organization's designated system, take notes, and set the tone and pace of the interview.

5. Exchange information with the other managers involved in interviewing. Gain consensus.

> ## *EXAMPLES OF SALES COMPETENCIES:*
> *initiative, innovation, tenacity, energy, organizational fit, results orientation, creativity, planning and efficiency, professionalism, building strategic relationships, concern for others, communication, persistence and diligence, ability to learn, ability to self-develop, self-awareness, teamwork, selling skills, maximizing opportunity, focusing on results, business acumen, and territory management.*

There are many more. Interviewers want to know if you possess these behaviors. Why? Because they are the behaviors of successful salespeople.

o Organizations use behavioral interviews because they are objective and specific to the position. Questions are predetermined and are generally formatted in an interview guide. From a legal perspective, organizations use behavioral interviews because the focus is skill, behavior, and result. It is an objective measure of the overall performance of a candidate, and it is job specific. It is not based on feeling or emotion, both of which are very subjective measures.

o Most interview guides use a comprehensive rating scale. The interviewer will rate each competency independently then give an overall rating. The interview remains objective because the same questions are asked of every candidate. The ratings are based on the candidate's ability to provide specific examples and answer the questions thoroughly. The higher the rating, the more likely the job offer or invitation to interview again. When two or more people interview, each interviewer will rate each candidate independently. However, the interviewers will come to consensus during debriefing. Generally, an average overall rating will determine the strongest and weakest candidates.

o STAR (**S**ituation, **T**ask, **A**ction, and **R**esult) is an acronym you need to commit to memory. The STAR format will help you answer behavioral questions. Remember, behavioral interviews are designed to draw out *specific* behavior, *specific* action and the ensuing *specific* result. It forces a specific answer to a question.

o Unfortunately, most candidates speak in generalities— "I would do this...," "I could do...," "I think I should do..." This is unacceptable in a behavioral interview. We want to know what *was* the situation, what actions *did you* take and what *was* your *result*. Notice the difference?

o How do you identify a behavioral question? Generally, a behavioral question begins with "Tell me about a time when...," "Tell me about a situation where you...," or "Can you give me an example of..., The questions are designed to determine how *you* acted in a certain **S**ituation, the **T**ask at hand, the **A**ctions *you* took and the **R**esult *you* achieved. A behavioral question elicits an experience. The key is to give a specific and relevant answer from your experience.

o Prepare your STAR examples in advance. Have many examples of specific situations. Using the same example throughout the interview conveys a lack of depth and critical thinking. Your examples must be honest and detailed. An interviewer can quickly identify a fabricated example and will ask you to provide another. When the interviewer asks several questions related to the original, he or she has doubt. Use relevant STAR examples to eliminate doubt.

o Make your STAR examples relevant to the job you are interviewing for. Use examples of sales calls and customer interactions whenever possible. Every sales call and customer interaction is a potential example.

o In your STAR example, the result doesn't always have to be positive. I look for the ability of a candidate to link his or her behavior to the result, regardless if it was good or bad. I also look for what the person learned from that situation. Be prepared to answer the questions "What did you learn?" and "If you could do it again, what would have done differently?"

o How do you "frame" your answer? It may help to repeat the question asked for clarity: "This was the situation and the task I needed to accomplish. I took the following action in order to...and these are the results I attained from my action." *(STAR format)* Of course you will describe your STAR in much greater detail. Most candidates are not specific. They describe a weak, non-relevant situation, then give a philosophy lesson of what they could do or what they would do rather than what they did. Every sales call and every customer interaction you have made in your career is potential example. Use them.

o You will separate yourself from your competition using the STAR technique. Trained hiring managers look for the connection between the action you took and the result you achieved. They are looking for behaviors, skills and abilities that will transfer to the position you are interviewing for.

o Ask if you answered the question to the interviewer's satisfaction or if you should give another example. Remember to link the result (good or bad) to your action.

o Why is there so much focus on behavior as opposed to skill? Generally, you cannot teach behavior. By and large, people do not change their behavior over time. Remember, the past predicts the future.

o Practice, practice, practice answering behavioral-type questions. Do not stray or give a philosophy lesson. Stay on message specific to the question. Behavioral interviews are the most difficult. If you are not prepared, you will fail.

Sample Behavioral Questions:

1. Can you provide an example of when you accomplished an important project or task with very limited resources? What were the circumstances? What did you do? What were the results?

2. Tell me about a situation where you went above and beyond the call of duty. What happened? Why did you do it? What was the result?

3. Give me an example of being in a situation where things were not going well and you turned it around. What did you do? Why did you do it? What was the outcome?

4. What was the most difficult task you've had to learn? What did you do to learn? What was the result?

5. What is a recent responsibility you have taken on? Why did you assume this responsibility?

6. Give me an example of when you worked the hardest and felt the greatest sense of achievement. What did you do? What happened?

7. Tell me about a recent frustrating experience. Why were you frustrated? What did you do? What were the results?

8. Tell me about your job search strategy. What actions have you taken? Results?

9. When did you feel the most significant achievement in a work situation? What did you do, and why was it so rewarding?

10. Tell me about a situation in which you were rejected. How did you handle the outcome?

11. What has been your greatest obstacle? How have you dealt with it? What was the result?

12. Give an example of when your work was criticized. What was wrong with it, and how did you deal with it?

13. Tell me about a time in the past year when you have been opposed in a discussion. How did you react?

14. Under what conditions and in what environment do you work best? Give specific examples.

15. How often is your schedule upset by unforeseen circumstances? Give me a recent example and how you handled it.

16. Tell me about procrastinating about a decision in the past six months. Why did you do what you did?

17. Tell me about a time you obtained information about a key competitor. Who was the competitor? How did you utilize the information gathered?

18. What steps have you taken to improve your performance? Give me an example of when you did this and why.

19. Tell me about a time you developed a new and creative idea to solve a business problem. How did you apply this approach?

20. Give me an example of how your selling techniques are different from those in your district or region.

21. Describe a time when you experienced organizational change. What was that change and how did you respond?

22. Tell me about your most successful sales call.

23. Tell me about a time when a sales call was interrupted by unforeseen obstacles. What were the obstacles, and what did you do?

24. Give me examples of sales approaches you use to sell different audiences.

25. Tell me about a sales call that you won versus a call you lost. What happened?

26. Tell me about a call you wish you could do over. What happened and what did you learn?

27. Tell me about a time when you were not pleased with your performance. What did you do to correct the situation?

28. Tell me about a time when your work was not up to the standards of your supervisor. What was the situation, and what action did you take as a result?

29. Give me an example of how you use creativity in your current position.

30. Give me an example of a time when you implemented coaching. Please provide the situation and the actions you took.

31. Give me an example of a time when you observed dishonesty in the workplace. What was the situation and the action you took?

32. Describe a situation where your product knowledge was challenged. What was the situation and what did you do?

33. Tell me about a decision you made that involved a great deal of risk. Why was it risky?

34. Tell me about a time when you sold a transactional product as opposed to a promotional product. What is the difference? How and why was your sales approach different? What were the results?

35. Tell me about a time you opened a new account.

o Review your résumé. What type of behavioral questions would you ask if you were the interviewer?

o Review your sales performance (past and present). What behavioral questions would you ask if you were the interviewer?

o Review your brag book and business plan. What behavioral questions would you ask if you were the interviewer?

There are hundreds more. You can conduct your own online research, but the thirty-five listed are the most common to the pharmaceutical, medical and biotech industry. Questions are multi-layered and designed to identify numerous competencies. I think you will agree the questions are not easy. As you prepare for your interview, take the time to develop your answers using the STAR format. Again, use many situations and specific examples to answer the questions. Recent examples are best, but relevant examples are a must. A note to medical and surgical device candidates: You must prepare examples that include a transactional selling process. The result should be specific to the task (goal) at hand.

Overall, the best advice I can give is to think about your current and previous experience, the results you obtained and the behaviors you exhibited to obtain them. Relate your skills and behaviors to the position you are interviewing for. Think about the questions an interviewer could ask and write them down. What is the competitive landscape, what are the managed care challenges, what changes in the health care environment created obstacles or opportunities? How did you perform and how long did it take, what was your market share versus others in your district and region, how did you rank, and why did you achieve the level of performance you did? These are just a few. You need to realize your behavior caused something to happen in the sales process. Your behavior caused a result.

"A prudent question is one-half of wisdom."
—*Francis Bacon*

SAMPLE QUESTIONS

There are hundreds of questions an interviewer can ask. I have included the industry's most common. Your goal: Be prepared for any and all of them. Preparation is the recurrent theme of this book. Take the time to write your answers in advance of the interview. Role-play with an objective friend, colleague, or family member. Many of these same questions could be asked during the phone screen or first face-to-face interview. Take advantage of the fact that you know the questions in advance. Be cautious. Do not over speak any answer. Be concise, be specific, be relevant, and be honest. Integrate past performance, past behavior, and how it produced results.

Many of the questions are actually not related to health care or the pharmaceutical industry. However, this is a professional sales position. Most of the questions are designed to uncover the candidate's ability to deliver sales results, regardless of the product. You will also find redundancy in the questions. This is by design. Hiring managers look for consistency and will ask the same question several different ways throughout the interview. Like you, a good interviewer prepares in advance.

60 Common Questions:

1. Tell me about yourself.
2. Why should I hire you?
3. How do you separate yourself from others you work with?
4. Why are you leaving your current employer?
5. Why did you select our organization to interview with?
6. How do you like to be managed?
7. What are your strengths and weaknesses?
8. How did you prepare for this interview?
9. Who else are you interviewing with?
10. What do you know about our company?
11. How do you set goals?
12. Define success.
13. What motivates you?
14. Why pharmaceutical, medical, or biotech sales?
15. What is it about sales you like?
16. What is your career path?
17. How do you overcome obstacles?
18. How do you organize your day, your week, and your month?
19. What drives you crazy about your current job?
20. What is your current salary and bonus?
21. What do like about your current manager?
22. What do you dislike about your current manager?
23. What are your salary expectations?
24. What are you most proud of?
25. Describe in detail your workday yesterday.

26. Did you attend college?

27. Why did you pick this school?

28. Did you work while in college?

29. Be prepared to answer why you left each employer for another.

30. This position provides a company car and requires proof of insurability at acceptable rates. How many moving violations have you had within the past three years?

31. All employees are required to take and pass a drug test. Are you okay with this requirement?

32. In order to offer employment, you will need to supply a copy of last year's W-2 or 1099 form to verify your income, a current pay stub and a copy of your college transcripts. Would you be able to do so? If you move on to a second interview, you may be required to bring those with you.

33. Our organization could potentially have similar openings across the nation. Are you willing to relocate at this time? To where? How about in the future?

34. How many nights are you comfortably and routinely able to spend away from home each month?

35. Are overnights and occasional weekend travel for sales meetings and conventions okay with you?

36. How are you accounting for your time during this interview?

37. Our training class requires ____ consecutive weeks in _____ including the weekend in between. Are you able to manage that?

38. What school-related extracurricular activities were you involved with, and what was your involvement?

39. What was your GPA? Make sure you know your overall GPA and the GPA in your specific major.

40. Why did you pick the major that you did?

41. Highlight your college experience for me. Tell me things such as your GPA, honors, awards, and/or achievements that you earned.

42. What were some of your toughest classes? What types of grades did you get?

43. What were your easiest classes? Why do you think those classes were easiest for you?

44. Thinking back through your college career, what do you consider to be your top accomplishment?

45. What do you like about working in pharmaceutical and health-care sales?

46. Why do you want to work in the health-care field?

47. What organizations are your currently looking at and why?

48. How would you describe yourself as a salesperson?

49. Tell me about your day yesterday, starting with the time and location of your first customer call and ending with your last work-related activity.

50. What is your method for tracking items that require your attention?

51. How much growth did your territory have this year over last? Why? To what do you attribute the change?

52. What are some ideas you have presented to your team members that were accepted by the group? What was your approach?

53. Have you ever helped a colleague improve his or her performance? Tell me about one of those times.

54. When dealing with team members, a customer or a group, how do you determine when you are pushing an issue or decision too hard? Tell me about a time when you pushed too hard.

55. Have you taken any recent steps to improve your skills or performance? Were they mandated by the company, or did you initiate these steps yourself?

56. What techniques and skills have you learned to make you more effective in your job? How did you learn them?

57. What was the greatest business obstacle in your territory this past year? What steps did you take to overcome these obstacles?

58. Have you ever launched a new product? If so, how did you prepare for that product launch?

59. Which information sources do you use to manage your territory? Can you provide an example of one source that you have found particularly effective and why? How have you measured the effectiveness of that source?

60. How long will it take you to make an impact and generate sales?

o Prepare for multi-layered questions. Multi-layer questions are designed to determine decision-making, judgment and consistency within your answer. Listen carefully to the interviewer as he or she asks additional questions directly related to your initial response. The interviewer is trying to uncover additional information. If the questions sound similar, they are for a reason. Provide more information but make sure it is connected to your original answer. A change or inconsistency may do more harm than good.

o Read body language and quickly assess the situation. If an interviewer expresses confusion, you must provide clarity. If he or she is stuck on one question and appears unsatisfied with your answer, there may be doubt. Doubt will separate one candidate from another. **Doubt is the enemy!**

○ Review your résumé. What questions would you ask if you were the interviewer?

○ Review your brag book. What questions would you ask if you were the interviewer?

○ Review your sales results and performance evaluations. What questions would you ask if you were the interviewer?

Of course, there are hundreds more. The interviewer will also have additional questions depending on your answers, so be prepared. The better you can prepare and anticipate a follow-up question, the better your chances of achieving your goals. Remember, long-winded dissertations are not acceptable. The interviewer will either stop listening or ask more questions. With the amount of information at your fingertips and the questions included in this guide, there should be no surprises. Always use specific examples, provide results attained, and make your answer relevant to the position you are interviewing for. You are now prepared for interview success.

"Common sense is not so common."

—*Voltaire*

A DAY IN THE FIELD

A day in the field is like a two-minute warning in football. Congratulations, you're getting close to victory but be careful, because much can go right and much can go wrong. A day in the field is code for **you have an eighthour interview**. Do not be over confident, drop your guard, or say things you wouldn't say during a regular interview. Use your common sense, exercise good judgment, and always accommodate the person you are working with. It is not this person's responsibility to accommodate your schedule.

A hiring manager will typically send the two best candidates to spend a day in the field. Almost always, the field day is conducted with the same salesperson. Make no mistake; you are being compared to the other candidate during your day in the field. Are you the "right fit" for the selling environment? You are not spending a day in the field with an ordinary sales representative either. The manager has chosen this sales rep because he or she exhibits the skills and behaviors necessary to be successful. The sales rep is a tremendous resource and should be treated with utmost respect. This person will observe and evaluate your professionalism, preparedness, interest, passion, desire, communication, intelligence, judgment, selling skills, and organization, to name a few, often using a checklist and evaluation form to remain objective. Of course, follow up immediately with a thank-you note.

More often than not, the field visit determines the best candidate for the position. I have eliminated excellent candidates who performed extremely well on their interview but exhibited poor behavior or judgment during their field visit. It is critical to exhibit a high level of professionalism, common sense, and good judgment. Spending a day in the field with a sales representative is relatively unique to the pharmaceutical, medical device, surgical and biotech industry. Employers have too much to risk and too many good candidates to wonder if their candidate will fit in their selling environment. A field day provides deep insight for the candidate and hiring manager.

o Remember, a field visit is an eight-hour interview. Do not assume you have the job because you have been asked to go on a field day. I have eliminated many candidates because of poor field days.

o Arrive early. Confirm your time and exact meeting place the day before. Being late is not an option.

o Program the contact information of the person you will be spending the day with in case you need to call them.

o Dress professionally. Apply the same dress principles as you would for the interview.

o Avoid strong perfume or cologne. Many people are allergic to fragrances. Be sensitive to the person you are working with.

o Never smoke in the vehicle or prior to making a sales call. I suggest not smoking during the entire day.

o Ask good questions. Prepare them in advance of the day. Questions should be pertinent to the position or organization.

o You do not have to be a wallflower. Be appropriate and professional in your level of engagement with customers. Discuss your role in advance.

o Be professional in offices. Do not make a situation uncomfortable for the customer or existing representative. Discuss what your role will be prior to each call.

o Do not swear, cuss or use any inappropriate language no matter how comfortable you feel.

o If you are an experienced salesperson, do not feel the field day is beneath you. It is a great opportunity to be part of and witness the actual selling environment.

o Be attentive and sensitive to the person you are working with. You are a guest. You are not in control of the radio or temperature of the vehicle you are riding in.

o Do not ask to be dropped off early. Let the representative you are with determine when your day is done. Accommodate the salesperson; he or she does not accommodate you.

o Take time off from your current employer when interviewing or conducting a field day. I ask candidates how they are accounting for their time during the interview. If the candidate flinches, they are out. I want to hire a truthful person.

o Send a thank you note immediately following your field visit.

"Trusting our intuition often saves us from disaster."
— *Anne Wilson Schaef*

ALWAYS & NEVER THE DO'S AND DON'TS OF INTERVIEWING

Simply stated, these are the best and worst practices gathered over the years. You just can't make this stuff up. Yes, I have had people drop the "f-bomb" during an interview. I suppose they felt a little *too* comfortable. If you do nothing else, take these suggestions and apply them. Quite often the simplest things separate one candidate from the next. Remember, never are two candidates equal, and doubt is the enemy. Again, the industry is too competitive to leave anything to chance, even the smallest detail. Your experience alone is not enough. Too many qualified candidates have not been hired because they broke some of the rules outlined in this guide.

Always means always, and never means never. In other words, these are not suggestions. Consider them mandates. You do not want to be the subject of a manager's interviewing "war story" by doing something foolish that could easily have been avoided. Many of the points are woven throughout the guide. Let these serve as a final reminder to take them seriously.

ALWAYS:

✓Always… Do your research and be prepared for the interview process.

✓Always… Practice and rehearse your answers prior to the interview.

✓Always… Focus on your ability to increase and improve sales results.

✓Always… Make yourself available for a phone screen, interview and field visit.

✓Always… Ask for the business cards of each person you interview with and provide yours if you have one.

✓Always… Send a thank-you e-mail or handwritten card to each and every person you interviewed with.

✓Always… Send a thank-you to the sales representative you spent a day in the field with. Copy the manager and send a separate e-mail to him or her as well.

✓Always… Follow up immediately on anything requested of you during the interview process.

✓Always… Be 100 percent truthful about every fact on your résumé.

✓Always… Write a results-focused résumé.

✓Always…Take responsibility and ownership for your performance.

✓Always… Use sales data to support performance and results.

✓Always… Be confident when discussing salary expectations.

✓Always… Be attentive and courteous of people's time.

✓Always… Be able to back up and discuss every fact and statement on your résumé.

✓Always… Turn off your cell phone during an interview—not vibrate, off. I suggest doing the same during the field visit.

✓Always… Turn off your Blackberry or other PDA device during the interview.

✓Always… Dress professionally and be well groomed.

✓Always… Contact your references prior to the interview. Obtain their permission, and make sure their contact information is accurate and up to date. Include their title on your reference sheet. Know what they will say when called.

✓Always… Provide multiple contact numbers for yourself.

✓Always… Make it easy for people to contact you.

✓Always… Spell-check and grammar-check everything you write.

✓Always… Know your strengths and weaknesses, and be prepared to discuss them.

✓Always… Know your current salary and bonus structure, and be able to explain it.

✓Always… Know your current market share and rank within your existing organization. Know how you are assessed, measured, and evaluated.

✓ Always… Ask for clarity of a question if you do not understand; ask but do not interrupt when your interviewer is speaking.

✓ Always… Let your performance make a statement, not your clothing.

✓ Always… Use "I" rather than "we" or "us" when answering results-related questions.

✓ Always… Take time off from your current employer when interviewing or during a field day.

✓ Always… Leave something behind after an interview—your brag book, 30-60-90 or basic business plan, etc.

✓ Always… Follow up immediately on any commitment you gave during the entire process.

✓ Always… Ask what the next steps are.

✓ Always… Ask when a decision will be made, when the company expects to inform you and how it will communicate the decision.

✓ Always… Do a Google search of your own name to see what your future employer may see on the Internet.

✓ Always… Close and ask for the job…**always.**

NEVER:

✗ Never… Fill silence with pointless chatter.

✗ Never… Lie or stretch the truth on your résumé or during any part of the interview process.

✕ Never… Speak negatively of a former employer.

✕ Never… Leave the interviewer wondering why you are leaving your current employer.

✕ Never… Conduct a phone screen on your cell phone while driving.

✕ Never… Make the interviewer adjust his or her schedule to meet your needs.

✕ Never… Lose focus or sight of the fact that you are interviewing for a sales position.

✕ Never… Eat or drink unless asked.

✕ Never… Create doubt in the mind of the interviewer.

✕ Never… Leave the interview without asking for the job.

✕ Never… Blame a partner, your manager, managed care, your competitor, your budget, your product, your customers, "the company," or anything else for poor sales performance.

✕ Never … Swear, cuss or use slang on an interview.

✕ Never… Discuss race, gender, age, religion, politics, etc.

✕ Never… Make any sexual references during the entire interview process.

✕ Never… Dress provocatively to an interview or during the field day.

✖ Never... Physically bring plaques, awards or trophies to an interview.

✖ Never... Chew gum or smoke.

✖ Never... Be late; there is no excuse.

✖ Never... Use the interview to find out more about the job. Unprepared job seekers never get hired.

✖ Never... Stalk or become a nuisance to human resources, the hiring manager, or anyone else in the organization. This includes multiple e-mails, repeated phone calls and text messages.

✖ Never... Are two candidates equal.

✖ Never... Have misspelled words on your résumé, thank-you notes, e-mails, job applications, or any other correspondence.

✖ Never... Use your résumé to write a job description.

✖ Never... Assume your previous experience will guarantee a call, an interview, or the job.

✖ Never... Give books or gifts to the interviewer. Although your intent may be good, it may cause more harm than good.

"To know what has to be done, then do it, comprises the whole philosophy of practical life."

—*Sir William Osier*

RESOURCES: WHERE TO FIND
WHAT YOU NEED

There are hundreds of websites you can reference for research. I have provided some of the most common industry sites. In my opinion, Linkedin, Indeed, MedReps, and Medzilla are among the best. MedReps does charge a small fee for candidates and recruiters, but I believe it is well worth it. Web-based research will provide a solid foundation of information and provide additional resources. Also, each company has its own dedicated website. Take the time to search through the entire site. A company website may prove to be the best resource you have. Print the information and organize it in a binder for reference. Many company websites include mission statements, history, news articles, management philosophy, and more. Where better than the company's own site to provide the specific information you need?

Google and Yahoo search engines are your friends, but they are not your only friends. Search key words, such as product names, disease state, hospitals, biotech, specialty pharmaceutical, health care sales, managed care, recruiters, local health-care landscape, medical device, pharmaceutical sales, etc. One search will beget another. It's important to use a variety of resources. Variety is the key to gaining a broad perspective. Research and preparation are vital to your success.

Take advantage of "people resources" including family, colleagues, friends, a local pharmacist, your family physician, recruiters, professors, etc. Have you ever considered calling the company you are interested in joining? Call them, seek information, request managers' names and contact information in the area where you live. I have been contacted by prospective candidates, and appreciate their "out of the box" thinking and proactive approach.

Do not underestimate the power of Linkedin. Linkedin has become one of the best research and recruiting websites available. We live in the information age. Take advantage of it. However, it does take time. Plan and schedule your research time. Brian Tracey says it best: "Your greatest resource is your time." I will say this one last time: Lack of preparation is the number one reason candidates are not hired. Your career is too important to leave to chance.

COMMON INDUSTRY and JOB SEARCH WEBSITES:

http://www.medzilla.com

www.medreps.com

www.cafepharma.com

www.topdogmedicalsales.com

www.napsronline.org
http://www.biospace.com/company_index.aspx

www.pharmaceutical-industry.info

NEWSWIRE PR TODAY™

NEWS DISTRIBUTION NETWORK

http://www.newswiretoday.com/news/15997/

http://www.medicare.gov

 U.S. Food and Drug Administration http://

www.fda.gov
http://www.monster.com

careerbuilder.com™

http://www.careerbuilder.com
www.hoovers.com
www.corporateinformation.com
www.interview.monster.com
www.job-interview.net
www.careerbuzz.com
www.careersite.com

one search. all jobs.

http://www.indeed.com/

Indeed.com is fast becoming one of the favorites because, as the logo reads, "one search all jobs." Type in your key words and away you go. Indeed pulls postings from all other sites. It is a tremendous time-saver. Three of the last five candidates I hired found the position through indeed. com.

http://www.linkedin.com/

Linkedin has become **one of the best recruiting websites** available and is the world's largest professional network with more than 150 million members. Take the time to create a profile, join the many professional groups within the site, and begin networking with family, friends, and business associates.

Made in the USA
Lexington, KY
09 April 2014